T0209849

ALMOST DIVORCED

Marriage Is Hard Work . . . Duuuhhh

JACKIE ARCHIE

WESTBOW
P R E S S®
A DIVISION OF THOMAS NELSON
& ZONDERVAN

Copyright © 2019 Jackie Archie.

All rights reserved. No part of this book may be used or reproduced by
any means, graphic, electronic, or mechanical, including photocopying,
recording, taping or by any information storage retrieval system
without the written permission of the author except in the case of
brief quotations embodied in critical articles and reviews.

This book is a work of non-fiction. Unless otherwise noted, the author
and the publisher make no explicit guarantees as to the accuracy of
the information contained in this book and in some cases, names of
people and places have been altered to protect their privacy.

WestBow Press books may be ordered through booksellers or by contacting:

WestBow Press
A Division of Thomas Nelson & Zondervan
1663 Liberty Drive
Bloomington, IN 47403
www.westbowpress.com
1 (866) 928-1240

Because of the dynamic nature of the Internet, any web addresses or
links contained in this book may have changed since publication and
may no longer be valid. The views expressed in this work are solely those
of the author and do not necessarily reflect the views of the publisher,
and the publisher hereby disclaims any responsibility for them.

Any people depicted in stock imagery provided by Getty Images are
models, and such images are being used for illustrative purposes only.
Certain stock imagery © Getty Images.

ISBN: 978-1-9736-5029-4 (sc)
ISBN: 978-1-9736-5030-0 (e)

Print information available on the last page.

WestBow Press rev. date: 01/14/2019

Dedication

First and foremost, I give all honor, glory, and praise to God, who is the head of my life. To my husband Al. We have been through a lot in our 30+ years. My beautiful daughters Deonne, Cyntahva, and Faith. Thank you all for giving me the freedom to go back to school, to find my gifts, and to write this book. You are my biggest supporters & I love you.

Contents

Introduction

Life is so short, and, in that short time, we have hundreds of choices to make. From pre-school until you take your last breath, we are put in a position to have to make numerous decisions about our life. What? When? Where? How? Who? Why? Just about every life choice fits into one of these questions. Your life up to this very minute is the equivalent of the choices you've made.

Life stops being fun real quick when you start reaping from bad choices. I hope that when it comes time to marry that you get the significance of the importance of the choice you make. Nevertheless, even when you make all the right decisions for all the right reasons, things can go badly.

We, as adults, have to honor our choices. Marriage is not a fly by night temporary activity we sign up for. Marriage is a lifelong commitment. The marriage commitment affects more than just two people. Be careful what you chose, when you chose, where you chose, how you chose, whom you chose, and why you chose. Marriage is hard work. You are two people with different mindsets, different backgrounds, different values, different everything and you thought it would be easy because you love each other. Now, that is funny!

It is not over until you quit. Let me help you fix it, strengthen it, and grow

....TOGETHER.

ALMOST DIVORCED

Chapter 1

Why Did We Get Married

"Do not lose sight of how you started"

Why did we get married? What were we thinking? Why did we decide to make such a permanent, lifelong decision? Were we crazy? No, we were in love. Remember how they looked on your wedding day? How they almost glowed? We thought, "This is the first day of the rest of my life." We loved the way you smiled. We loved the way you laughed. We loved your eyes. We could not sleep when you were not there and when we did sleep you filled our dreams. Our love was so fulfilling that it stole our appetite. The list goes on and on of the things we said we could not live without.

That first year of marriage, the "Honeymoon Phase," we could do no wrong. This is where we found out all those things we hid while we were dating. Like we really can't cook; we only clean up after ourselves on Friday; we snore; our feet stink really badly after work; we don't wash dishes; we don't, we don't, we won't, we won't, and we can't, we can't. Nevertheless, for some reason during this phase it is all good. We could do no wrong. We actually thought all these new idiosyncrasies were adorable. This is where we found out things are not at all what they seemed to be or how we thought they would be. However, the sex is good; we are dancing in the rain, eating breakfast in bed, and our love covered a multitude of misguidings. Basically, we just didn't care, nor did we sweat the small stuff.

Now, after many fights, schedule clashes, missed

dinners, the kids took away date night, the trash never gets taken out anymore until the house reeks of it, sex is maybe once a month, and I know there's much much more, we say they've changed. It is not the same anymore. We want something different, something new, something fresh; we look at each other like there is just no more spark, and we ask ourselves, "Why did we get married?"

Look Dummy, different, new, fresh, and that spark are right in front of you. Even if you have only been married for two years, your spouse has changed. They ARE different, they ARE new, they ARE fresh, and the spark IS there, but it is up to you to see it, to recognize it, and to keep it ignited. **Those of you who are looking for different, new, and fresh are usually looking too much at everyone but your spouse.** I am sorry that was harsh. But, how harsh is it for you to think that suddenly that person who devoted their life to you isn't good enough anymore.

With every experience you have in marriage there is change and you get to be a part of it. Just like watching your child grow from infancy, to toddler, to adolescent, to teen, to young adult, and finally adult, you are amazed at the transformation. You admire their growth, and you celebrate their aging. However, when it comes to your spouse you are not so amazed; the admiration is gone. And why is that? The growth in your spouse as they go from single adult, to married, to parent, to empty nester, to retired, and to elderly is just as amazing.

When you have your first child, you are blessed to watch as they hold them fresh from birth with tears of joy in their eyes. You are blessed to watch their heart soften as they raise that baby, teaching and molding them into a little person; seeing this over and over again with every child.

Seeing the transformation from just your spouse evolving into this parenting machine, balancing schedules, supporting you as they also support the children. Watching them as they juggle games, practices, dinners, birthday parties, sicknesses, and tears. There is nothing sexier than watching their strength as they deal with the rampage of that crazy teenager with the ease of a professional boxer. They know when and where to hit, when to dodge and weave, when to go down, and when to throw that knockout punch all in love.

So what, the alone time with your spouse is less breathtaking but more meaningful and fulfilling. So what, the time with your spouse doesn't last as long as it used to. Honey, I would take 20 minutes of my husband loving being with me and holding me than 45 minutes of craziness then snoring 2 seconds later.

When people own fine, expensive art, they love explaining the cracks and nicks because with each one they know it only makes their piece of art more valuable. The more knowledgeable they are of these imperfections, the more confidence people have in them as art connoisseurs. I remember when my husband got his first gray hairs; it was when he lost his grandmother that they first started to appear right on the edges. As our oldest daughter started becoming a teenager, gray started to appear in his beard and just a few fine wrinkles were noticeable at the outer corners of his eyes. I remember thinking how distinctive and handsome he looked with age. When our other two daughters were born, his gray just went wild. Why would I look down at that? Why would watching the effects of life, our life, on my spouse's body suddenly not be attractive to me anymore? I am responsible for some of those effects. I am physically and mentally a part of those effects. No one else in this world has my mark, by choice, but my spouse. Now, that is mind-blowingly AMAZING.

How often do you study your spouse? What's their favorite color, food, movie? What are their fears? What are their dreams? Why do they always watch love stories or read romantic novels? Is it because they love a good love story, or is it the only romance they get because you don't have or make time? Why do they always seek out excitement or danger on the big screen? Is it because they are bored? Did anyone ever tell you that just living in the same house, taking care of kids, putting together your finances, walking the dog, going to work, and coming home every night doesn't make a great relationship, and it won't make your marriage strong? Listen, if you go to work every day, you show up on time, you put in the work but you never talk to anyone, you are going to miss a lot. The things that make a strong marriage have nothing to do with the house, the kids, or the dog. It has everything to do with you and your spouse alone. I do not mean alone in a room, but your marriage is only as strong as you and your spouse's personal relationship. If you do not really know them because outside of the bedroom you do not get to know them, you do not study them, you do not work on the relationship, when hard stuff comes up there's no glue holding you together. That is why so many marriages unravel when life gets hard. They are so focused on the marriage stuff, that after a few years, they do not know each other anymore.

If you wake up one day and suddenly your voice is gone, can your spouse speak for you? If you go out to a restaurant, can your spouse order your meal? Could they go out and buy you an outfit? Can they take care of you without you being able to say a word? Would your spouse know without a shadow of a doubt that you love them without you being able to say a word? If your answer to any of these questions is no, why not? The only person that should know you better than your spouse is God. Your spouse is your fine piece of art. You should know all the cracks and nicks your spouse possess because you understand that each one makes your spouse more valuable. The more knowledgeable you are of these imperfections, the more confidence your spouse will have in their value to you. How can you love me if you do not even know me? How can you love me if you are not always studying me and knowing me? Sit down and ask yourself, "Why did I get married?" This question is not to spawn reasons to get out but to get better and do better.

ALMOST DIVORCED

CHAPTER 2

What Does Love have to do with it?

"Love is not an emotion. It is an action"

Love is not an emotion. It is an action. Do not misunderstand me. Love is needed in a relationship. Once you are married, love isn't the fluttery feeling you get when you see your spouse across the room, when they get so close you can feel their warm breath on the back of your neck, or how you feel after a long passionate night of love making. That is lust. Lust is good, but it does not equate to love.

Love is a choice. Love is what makes you stand before your family, friends, a clergy or justice of the peace and promise before God that you will be a true and devoted spouse, true in sickness and in health, in joy and in sorrow, in prosperity and adversity; and, forsaking all others, you will keep yourself for your spouse, and for your spouse only, in all love and honor, in all duty and service, in all faith and tenderness, to live with them and cherish them according to the ordinance of God, until death us do part.

Love is staying with your spouse when they lose all the finances. Love is saying "NO" when someone throws himself or herself at you sexually, even when everything in you wants to say "YES". Love is honoring your spouse by being honest in all things, fair and respectful. Love is representing your family at home and when you are away. Love is treating your spouse with kindness and letting your actions show how you feel. Words are easy and, even though your spouse will want to and needs to hear you say you love them, it means absolutely nothing to hear it if they do not also feel loved.

Look, my spouse gets on my last nerves and we have had some really rough times, but I made a decision when I married to have stick-ability. I do not want an out. I really do love my spouse. All emotions aside, why would I want to start over again? Good and bad, my spouse knows me better than anyone besides God. Why would I want to run the risk of going through the same hardships, and yes I said hardships, again? I have a 99.9% chance that there are some things I will never go through again in my relationship with my spouse. I say 99.9% because there are no 100% guarantees. If my spouse did something that really hurt me, if my spouse watched me spiral out because of something he did, it is very likely he will not do that to me again. The same goes vice versa. Getting with someone new, you are guaranteed to go through many of the same awful experiences again or worse experiences; and honey, life is too short.

Is my spouse perfect? No, but neither am I. I chose to stay in love because I want to. Sure, I could look for someone else. Sure, I could find someone better. So can my spouse. There is always better out there. There is always worse as well. You can get what you want, but is it worth losing what you have? My answer is a sound NO it is not. Starting over is highly overrated.

Your kids do not always come out as you would like,

but we do not just throw them to the side and start over. Where's the guarantee in that method? It is no different with your spouse. Where's the guarantee that the second one will be any better or not worse than the other will? The grass always looks greener on the other side, but we forget that crab grass is green too. We forget that salt looks just like sugar.

We say our children are a part of us. What! You think your spouse is not a part of you? When you stood before God and exchanged vows, you became one with your spouse. Even when a marriage separates, they are still forever connected. That connection may be hate, but it is still a connection. Why do you think divorced couples sometimes spend their entire lives hating or being mad at each other? They stay connected till death whether they want to or not. My parents were married for 28 years before they got divorced. My mom passed away in 2014, but while she was in the hospital, my dad visited her often. My mom, while in the hospital, asked my sister and me how we felt about her and our dad getting back together. We laughed because we knew she was a little out of it because of what she was going through medically, but they were still connected. My siblings and I are grown; he did not have to continue a relationship with her, but my dad was still connected to my mom. She was every bit a part of him as his kids. My dad still holds a special place in his heart for my mom. What I am trying to say is: when you make that deep connection with someone that is so heart felt that you desire to spend the rest of your life with them, you marry them and start a life together, that doesn't just go away because you get mad or unsatisfied.

Look, marriage is hard, constant work. It is the hardest thing you will ever do. Has anyone ever told you that you will not always like your spouse? Well, it is true. Right now, as I am writing this, I do not like my spouse very much. You are probably thinking, "good grief how can you give me advice about my marriage?" I can because 1. I have been married to the same person for over 30 years and 2. Just because I give marital advice does not mean I do not have marital problems. My spouse and I have been "Almost Divorced" before. We have many of the same problems other marriages have. My marriage is not an exception to the rule. Do you think that grief counselors have never grieved, doctors never get sick, and surgeons never have surgery? Maybe it is easier to believe counselors have it all together. Well, we do not. We just have a gift to help others. We have to make the same choices you do about our spouse. We all have to choose to stay and fight.

When we were a new married couple, every time we got into a huge fight someone would always bring up leaving. I was so glad when we finally got to a maturity that, even in rough times, nobody is going anywhere. You cannot work on problems if you are always afraid someone was walking out. This is when you start to really love your spouse. When you make up in your mind that this is it. We are either going to be good together or bad together but together it is. Some would say this is stupid. No, this is marriage. You and your spouse get to decide what it is going to be. You can stay in the bad you are in or you can work it out.

Marriage is no different from any other relationship in regards to needing to be cultivated to keep it healthy. Someone is always going to make a mistake, say the wrong thing, forget a birthday or anniversary, or hurt you, but you have to remember that you did not marry a perfect person. Just as sure as they are going to mess up, you are going to mess up too.

I tell my kids all the time, "no matter what you do, I may not like it, but I will always be your mother." That is no different from what you told your spouse on your wedding day. In short, you said, "no matter what you do, I may not like it, but I will always be your spouse." You were not just saying something to be cute. You gave a vow to your spouse and to God in front of the world. A vow is a solemn, earnest declaration. Solemn means you gave it serious thought. Earnest means serious in intention. Declaration is an announcement or proclamation. Those vows are the reason that marriage is not to be taken lightly. Hence, the question, what does love have to do with it? Take real ownership in your marriage and do what needs to be done to fix it, strengthen it, and grow together.

CHAPTER 3

Marriage is a Two-Way Street

"Kick down your ONE-WAY sign and pick up a MERGE"

There are no I's in team, but there is an I right smack in the middle of marriage. So, you have to be careful not to get so stuck on yourself that you forget you have another half. I want this! I want that! I, I, I; this can no longer be in your vocabulary when you are married. Do not get me wrong, you can and must take care of yourself and have some me-time but marriage is a partnership. Everything you do from the time you say "I do" affects your spouse in either a positive or a negative way. The moment you start thinking it is my way or the highway, just know that your marriage is in deep trouble.

If you have a spouse that goes along with this "all about you" program, just give it time. They are going to wake up one day so devastatingly unfulfilled that they are going to hate their life, and they are going to hate you. If you have a spouse that does not go along with this "all about you" program, both of you are going to be continuously butting heads. You will be always pushing against each other until you tear each other apart. Either way, it is definitely a loose loose situation.

What makes you think that your wants and dreams are more important than your spouse's wants and dreams? Remember growing up with all kinds of ideas and visions for how you wanted your future to turn out? Well, your spouse grew up having all kinds of ideas and vision for their life as well. How dare you think they are just here to subsidize your life, your vision? Now on the flip side, if you don't let your dreams be known and only live for your spouse's dreams, you are going to one day find yourself very unfulfilled, unhappy, and resentful. Do you realize that it is very possible for you both to live out your dreams together with each of you in support of the other? Two fulfilled dreams coming together in unity is what makes a power couple.

How you raise your kids, every decision made should be a shared experience. Sure, it is okay to have a head of household but that position is not a dictatorship. Some spouses out there really do drink their own Kool-Aid. They really believe their spouse is there just to support them and what they want. And what they want is the all-important way of life. They throw some accolades their spouse's way to make them feel okay for doing it their way, but at the end of the day, it is pure, unadulterated selfishness.

I know there are jobs that do take precedence due to their importance, like being President or a Bishop, but there is still room to allow your spouse to fulfill their dreams. The First Wife has an agenda of her own, and she pursues her agendas. There are wives of Bishops who have careers while they support their husbands.

It **IS** a two way street, but it has to be purposeful. We cannot be so busy pushing our own agenda that we lose sight of the fact that our spouses are people too. As passionate as you are about whatever it is you do, you have to know that your spouse has passions too. How would you feel if someone came along one day and cut off your passion? Well, this may very well be what you are doing to your spouse. If you are okay with that, there is a huge problem in your marriage but, more importantly, that level of selfishness is a character flaw.

People need to be fulfilled. Your spouse had a long life before you came along. Just because they fell in love with you does not mean they have to give up all the dreams they had many many years before they said "I do." If a person agrees to marry you at 25 years of age, how can you squash 25 years' worth of dreams? When you say "I do," you share your life; you do not give up your life. If you are making your spouse give up their entire 20 something years of dreams, first, shame on you, and second, show your spouse that they are as important as you are by sharing their life, not disregarding it.

Dictatorships cause you to miss everything your spouse is. You are hindering their purpose. Gifts come to everyone. I am sure your spouse's gift is not just to take care of your wants and needs. Talk about drinking your own kool-aid! YOU make it yourself! YOU make your spouse serve it to you! YOU dare them to drink any, and YOU every now and then let them have some! All I can say is: WOW!

You are missing out on the best part of marriage. Do you worry what will happen to your spouse when the kids are gone or when you retire? Or, in your mind, will they become a fulltime maid and servant? They wake up to fix you breakfast, sit in wait to see what you want for lunch, then dinner and desert of your choosing. Days just full of: what do you want honey? That is just SAD. If you do not have a desire to see your spouse fulfill any of their dreams and want to do as much for them as they do for you, honey, you are going to one day choke on your own kool-aid.

A spouse should want to see all their spouse has to offer. They may want to start a business, continue their education, volunteer, work part time, so they can have some money of their own, learn a craft, cultivate a hobby, or just explore life to see where they fit in it. I have been married for over 30 years, and I have three beautiful daughters. However, I am more than just a wife. I am more than just a mother. Because my husband encouraged me to explore my dreams, I have increased my education. I learned that I am a great teacher. I paint great pictures. I play guitar. All these things make me an even better wife and mother. I am confident and have a lot to offer.

In a marriage, spouses should make each other better. I should increase my husband and my husband should increase me. What kind of life is it if I increase my husband and he just tolerates or just humors me? It is lopsided and, more importantly, somebody is in pain.

If you take a baby and bound them so tight that they have no room to grow, they are going to be deformed and eventually will die. If you take your spouse and bound them so tight that they have no room to grow, they are going to be deformed and eventually will die.

We are all created to do and be something that has nothing to do with our spouse. My gaining higher education, painting, and playing the guitar really have nothing to do with my spouse, but my spouse benefits from all of it. My gifts increase us. When my husband goes out and fixes something or constructs something, it has nothing to do with me, but I benefit from him. Alone we are great but together we are AWESOME!

If apart from you and your agenda, your spouse is nothing and has nothing then you should be ashamed. You should desire your spouse to have a fulfilled life as you have. You also have to ask yourself, why are you okay with your spouse being less fulfilled? Moreover, if you really think your spouse is happy and has no dreams, ask them. Ask them if there is something, they want more for their life than to be your spouse. Ask them what their lifelong dreams are. Ask them what kind of dreams and ambitions they had for their life before they met you.

Now, ask yourself, what you are going to do when you find out they have dreams and desires outside of you? Are you going to continue allowing them to drink from your cup or encourage them to have a cup of their own? Loving someone can be very freeing or it can be a prison. When your spouse walks into their home, do they see the sky or are they looking at bars?

ALMOST DIVORCED

CHAPTER 4

It is Okay to Argue

"Agree to disagree"

A spouse that says they never argue is a spouse who is saying they do not want to communicate. In addition, I bet if you ask some detailed questions, you will find that that same spouse doesn't communicate about much of anything. But, they will say their marriage is fine. You will also find their spouse to be very unhappy, and will tell you nothing ever is settled, and their marriage is nowhere near fine.

Does this scenario sound familiar? I hope not, but, if it does, you can turn it around by just communicating. Most spouses know what is wrong in their marriage but their pride will not let them fix it. Why is this so hard? This is your spouse, the person who knows you best, the one who sticks it out with you, but you do not want to fix hurt and pain. I would question whether this spouse really loves their spouse. This sounds to me like a spouse that is going along for the ride because they have nothing better to do and would rather be in a bad marriage than have to deal with the stigma of divorce or too much of a coward to leave. So let us just stay, do nothing, and make everyone miserable because you cannot get it together and be a loving spouse.

If your child was in the middle of the road hurt and bleeding, would you just leave them there? And, even worse, would you stand there every day and look at them, watch the life leaving them? Would you sit back and say, "It was there fault. They had no business in the road. They should have been more aware of their surroundings. Why were they in the road in the first place?" You would not ask any of those questions if you saw your child in the middle of the road! No! You would run out there and do everything you could to save them. You would scream and holler until you got some help, and at the very least, if you saw that they were going to die and there was nothing anyone could do, you would hold them and love on them right in the middle of the road until they took their last breath.

But your spouse, you just leave them? Alone, hurting, bleeding, dying, and you stand there, watching. No screams for help, no desperation, just nothing, but you say you love them. You said, "in sickness and in health." You said, "in joy and in sorrow, in prosperity and adversity; and forsaking all others, in all love and honor, in all duty and service, in all faith and tenderness, to live with them and cherish them according to the ordinance of God, until death us do part."

In the thick of it, you changed it to, "I will do what I feel, and, if I do not want to, I won't, if I do, I will. I am not responsible for you; you are on your own, and I will help you, if it does not make me feel bad or inconvenience me, and, if you do not like it, you can leave so I will not look bad." WHAT THE WHAT????

Getting involved, looking out, ARGUING, and communicating is just you staying engaged. When your spouse wants to go to Alaska for vacation and you do not think a vacation is anywhere cold, say so. When you hold back what you feel, you hold back who you are from the person who needs to know you more than anyone does. What is wrong with arguing? Being passionate about something makes you feel alive and it is sexy.

Being married does not mean giving up who you are. When you reveal yourself and your spouse reveals themselves, it is then that you flow. Like a stream, you flow. Close your eyes and imagine a stream as it flows, the unified sound of the water. The water clashing against the rocks or other obstacles in the water but nothing stops the flow.

That steady flow is why you can drink the water. Nothing negative can stay and take root because the flow is too strong and continuous. This is how a good marriage should be. We clash against rocks and other obstacles, but we keep flowing.

The moment a stream stops at the rocks or any other obstacle (when it is difficult), it ceases being a stream. The moment you stop engaging in your marriage, you cease having a marriage and you become two people living in the same house with no movement. When there is no flow, you have now become a stagnant pond.

Pond water cannot be ingested because it will make you sick from all the alga, waste, and disease. A stagnant marriage will make each party sick from all the dissatisfaction, the wasted years, and the wounds it causes.

Arguing does not equate to being mean. Since we were children, we learn that when you are losing an argument, you bring out the big guns.

Me: It is my turn,
You: No, it is mine,
Me: No, it is not, you just went,
You: Well well, you are ugly and you stink,
Me: Runs away crying.

This is not a win. When you are mean during an argument and leave your spouse hurt or crying, nobody won the argument. There was nothing accomplished but distance and mistrust.

Arguing is about one side trying to get the other to see their point of view. That is it. When this cannot happen just agree to disagree. Do not pull out the big guns on your spouse. You can say, "Honey, we are not going to agree on this one, so what can we do to compromise?"

We do not stop being grown-ups when we argue. We show our maturity when we argue and our pride. In addition, we show our spouse how important they are. Being mean during an argument is telling your spouse that if you make me mad or disagree with me, I will hurt you. Now we no longer have a safe environment. This is not good.

Label any area you are both in at the same time as "Nice Zones" This does not mean you cannot argue or get upset, but you cannot be mean. Labeling seems a little immature, but it will remind you to watch your emotions and your words. It will remind you that biting, scratching, and name-calling are not required to have an argument. No big guns required.

This is your person, just talk it out. It is okay to get frustrated, to get angry, even to get mad but never get mean. Meanness destroys trust and causes fatal wounds, and it will cause your spouse to not feel loved anymore.

Have you heard of couples having an argument then having great make-up sex later that day? It is because they still maintained that "this is my person". We do not always agree, but we are always in love. You can never lose sight of this, even in an argument.

In life, you have very few people who will love you regardless. This is a very small group called family. Spouses love you by choice. They have no connection to you, except they have opened their heart and chose to love you. This has to be purposeful every day.

We have to make sure every day that our spouses know we love them. Not every other day, every week, every month, or on their birthday and holidays but every day. This is not too much to ask from the person you gave your life to, and who gave their life to you until death us do part. Who else better? So, argue, get it all out, and continue to be passionate and loving before the argument, during the argument, and after the argument.

Argue, engage, feel, learn, know your spouse, and let

your spouse know you. Your marriage will be destroyed from your lack of .... You fill in the blank. I am not saying that you have to be perfect. Marriage does not require perfection; it just requires attention.

CHAPTER 5

Communicate

"If you do not talk to one another, you may as well pack up and leave"

D o you ever wonder how your parents knew what to get you for Christmas? When you opened that gift that you dreamed of all year, how did they know? It was communication. Do you have a child that literally talks your ear off? In your mind, you are screaming Ughhhh, but your heart is learning who they are through their communication. You learn who they want to be, what they like, what they dislike, their fears, their dreams, their insecurities, and their personality. I know to get my daughter a U of L women's basketball jersey because that team is all she talks of. Did she ask for a jersey? No, but through communication I know her.

Knowing your spouse's feelings and thoughts allows you to know how to love them. Some need words of affirmation, some need gifts, some need acts of kindness, some need touch, some need a few minutes of space each day, and some need attention, but, if you do not share yourself through communication your spouse could be loving you the wrong way, leaving you very unsatisfied, and vise versa.

Those spouses who do it their way and those spouses who always say, "Whatever you want" are missing out on an opportunity to learn about their spouse. They are missing an opportunity to engage. For example, planning a vacation, even if you do not care where you go, you and your spouse can spend hours looking at vacation websites, pamphlets, and brochures. This can be a lot of fun, and you can learn a lot. You can learn that your wife has insecurities about her body when she mentions she would never wear a bathing suit since she had a baby. You could make a mental note to mention how great she looks when she is in her panties getting ready for bed. She would never link the two, but you just took something you learned and loved her with it. A wife could learn in looking at vacations that her husband has always wanted to snorkel and on one of their trips she could just happen to choose a hotel that has snorkeling. What a coincidence? She just loved on him.

Communication is the door to the soul, the door to the mind, and the door to the heart of your spouse. Why would you not want to go through that door every chance you get?

Communication is the only way you and your spouse can know each other. What you like, what you dislike, what your fears are, what makes you smile, what you like or dislike about your spouse can only be known through communication. Communication is the heart and soul of a marriage.

Non-communication in a marriage causes bad things to happen. Non-communication allows the mind to wander. This is dangerous. Never leave your spouse to his or her own devices. Once you have a wrong idea in your head, it is next to impossible to remove it.

It is equivalent to taking the wrong exit on the highway. It may be many many miles before another exit comes up where you can turn around. Or worse, have you ever gotten off on an exit to turn around and realize that exit has no turn around exit, and you are really lost. This is non-communication.

Until you learn to communicate, you and your spouse are always going to be lost on the highway. With that being said, I get it; how do you communicate when you have not been communicating? Are you ready........ You just start communicating! Yes, you are going to fumble around and feel incredibly stupid, but your spouse will just think you look cute and they will appreciate your fumbled attempts. As you continue to communicate, you will get better and more confident. You will see how nice it feels for your spouse to know and understand you.

You should have a meaningful conversation with your spouse every day. And look, a conversation does not have to be an hour long. It only takes a few minutes out of your 24-hour day. Every other day you should reveal a moment that really meant something to you. Whether it made you angry, happy, sad, or uncomfortable, it does not have to be about your spouse. It could be something that happened to you at work, in the car, or anywhere.

You should share your life with your spouse. We spend a lot of hours away from our spouses. We are 8 hours at work, some longer, 5-6 days a week. We have other activities in life as well. And, when you do the math, we have very little meaningful time together. And, we have not even thrown in the kids and their schedules.

Let your spouse in on your day because it is also their day. This way your together even when you are apart. OH MY! OH MY! Did I just described....... INTIMACY. Intimacy is not dirty talking on the phone, flowers, and candy. Honey, intimacy is about COMMUNICATION. When you let your spouse into your world, show them all the soft and squishy places of your heart, the sex will come and it will be GOOOOOOOOOOOOD.

I hear you saying; No way; is it that easy? Now hear me when I say, YES IT IS. Try it! Communication is sexy. Turn off the TV, get some snacks, and have an all-out talk fest. Talk about work, the kids, the car, the house, your wardrobe. Not just the bad stuff but your fears, dreams, something that made you laugh, something that almost made you cry, and do not hold back. Then, be an active listener to their stuff.

Being an active listener is being engaged and attentive. Repeat back not just what they said but what you heard. Do not always be ready to give a quick fix answer because sometimes they are just wanting an ear to vent.

Communication is also physical. Touch your spouse. When you are walking in a store or in the car together, hold their hand. Occasionally bring it to your mouth and kiss the back of their hand. For no reason. When you are watching TV together, rub their leg or put your hand on their thigh. Do not be sexual, just be there and physical. This communicates that you still want them and love your choice in marrying them. If you only do these things when you want sex, it lessens their value. It becomes: you are only doing this because you want something, not necessarily because you love me.

Verbal communication lets you spouse **know** you love them. Non-verbal communication lets your spouse **feel** you love them. Verbal is as important as non-verbal and neither work well alone. Communication is the key that opens all the doors to your spouse's heart and soul. So, communicate with your mouth, your emotions, your hands.

ALMOST DIVORCED

CHAPTER 6

Fix it & Re-Connect

"It is NEVER too late"

No matter how hurt you or your spouse are, something inside wants nothing more than to reconnect. However, it has to start somewhere. One of you has to get the ball rolling. The connection between husband and wife is powerful. It is so powerful that even in disconnect mode there is still electricity, and, once reconnected, the power will flow as great as before the disconnect. You do not believe me? Try it.

Why is it so hard for people to humble themselves? Something has got to give. If you did something to break the bond between you and your spouse, it does not matter the reason, you have to **step up**. Why is it so easy to mess up but so hard to clean up?

Think of it like this: you risked everything to get or do what you wanted. Everything! Your spouse, your children, your family, your respect, your dignity all for what, a moment? For example, you had an affair. This other person has not committed themselves; to you, they have not promised you anything; there is no devotion, just sex. You risked it all for them. You were willing to lose everything for them. But for your spouse, you will not do what it takes to fix what you broke.

Why do they get your devotion and not your spouse? You will give up your spouse for a moment of pleasure, but you will not give up your pride for the spouse that wants to forgive you? You really expect them to clean up your mess and not complain about it? You want them to get on their hands and knees and clean up the filth of your indiscretion and get up and give you respect, give you love, give you devotion as if nothing happened? If you do this, all your spouse will ever see is the mess you made. Every time they look at you all they will ever think is what you would not do for them. When you tell them you love them, how can they believe you when you made them get down in your filth and clean up your mess? When you tell them they look handsome or beautiful, all they hear is how they were not good enough. This will forever cloud their view of you. And you are right, it is not fair but how fair, is it for them to clean up after you?

So, you throw your hands up and say, "well then, what can I do now?" Well, it is never too late. Just start over. I can hear you, "What! It has been days, weeks, months, or years." So what? What does time mean? So imagine this, stab your spouse in the heart, get them no medical treatment, then leave, come back in about a year, and see what condition they will be in. That is stupid. Right, because they will be dead or, at the very least, their life will be greatly altered because they will be in need of a heart transplant, right?

Mental wounds can cause as much damage. We see it all the time in children that have horrible parents or have a tragic life experience that messes up the rest of their life, but you think your spouse should do what when you inflict a deep emotional wound on them.

They should just get over it because time has passed. Are you even beginning to see the ridiculousness of this way of thinking?

Oh yeah and one more thing, you do not get to inflict pain and control the effect it has. WOW, how ingenious is that? Have you ever had a child that did something wrong and thought that because you waited until the next day to punish them the punishment would not be so bad? Most parents think this is hilarious. Time does not change what you did so why should it change the punishment?

Fix it! You cannot change what happened but meet them wherever they are and go from there. Act like it is the first day that it happened and start over because in their heart, time has stood still not because they will not let it go but because you wounded them and then just left them there alone.

Once you do this, you can begin to heal, **together**. You see, in marriage the word together means everything. If I wanted to get through stuff alone I would have stayed single. The together is what makes your stream flow. If you had done this immediately after the mistake, it would have been like a stream hitting the rocks and obstacles; you would have continued to flow. But, remember with flowing water comes pressure and no matter how long you dam up a stream, when that dam is released the water continues to flow. I am just asking you to get rid of the dam in your marriage. It will not be easy, and it will not be quick, but it will be worth it.

When skin is destroyed, it can still heal. However, it will not look or feel the same, but it is stronger and tougher. Mistakes are written into your greatness. Mistakes were not meant to destroy you but to make you stronger and tougher. Your marriage can actually come out stronger and tougher, or you can sit there and do nothing and your marriage will die.

For those who have been hurt, look it happened and you stayed. If your spouse is genuinely going above and beyond to try and clean-up the mess, I do not mean jumping through hoops, but genuinely doing all they can - Communicating, talking about it, how it affected you, how they feel about it, answering the why, explaining the best they can where they were mentally, seeking counseling for the both of you, I mean really trying. Give them some grace. Acknowledge what they are attempting. It will not be a quick process, and do not rush it. But when they have done all they can do, if it continuously goes unnoticed, they will quit trying.

Look, your spouse messed up, but remember, it is not how we fall; it is how we get up that matters most. They may end up being a better spouse, a better parent, a better everything. When someone almost loses something precious, they usually hold on to it even tighter; they appreciate it so much more. If they do not, you have to wonder if it really meant anything in the first place.

God help if you ever make a mistake and fall into temptation. You will want your spouse to show you some grace. But do not make it easy. I do not mean make it harder for them, but, if the heaviness of what they have done is not felt, it may change the outcome. Heal with your spouse, jump back on board and flow strong and continuous. But, no matter how much you love your spouse, do not jump in a pond of stagnant water because then you both will emotionally die.

Forgiveness is not for them only, it is also for you.

For those who do not have infidelity or physical abuse. I have to single those out because those two things cause heart wounds. Until those wounds are dealt with you cannot move forward.

Those are not the only things that hinder the marriage. You may have grown apart, argue all the time, never have sex, disagree on how to raise the children; the list can go on and on. The work is the same. You have to start over, but you both have to work and give 100%. By starting over, I do not mean getting remarried but rekindling the flame. Start small, like having a date night at home once a week by watching a movie together, take a walk in the park and just talk about anything but your problems, or the house, or the bills, or the kids. Talk about your dreams, about your plans for the future.

Wash the dishes, fold clothes, or play a game together. Send the kids away, pull a mattress in the living room, go out and by junk food and spend the weekend watching comedies, love stories, adventure movies, and talk. Take a dance class together; anything to start the re-connection process.

If it runs deeper than that, seek out marriage counseling. Going to counseling is not a sign of weakness. It is actually a big sign that you are willing to do whatever it takes to fix your marriage and sometimes an outside perspective is just what you need.

Fixing your marriage is like standing on a staircase. It is your choice which direction you go, up or down, or you can just sit there and do nothing. But, do not get mad if every time you look up you have not gone anywhere and everything is the same. That is like getting in the car to go somewhere but never starting it up, just sitting there expecting to move when you have not done anything. Sure being in the car does mean you want to go, but just sitting there proves you do not want to put in the work.

Re-connect is an action word. To re-connect the TV, you have to get up and plug it in. To re-connect to a family member, you have to pick up the phone and call or get up and go visit them. You have to do something. You cannot just sit there and expect change to just happen. You may think that time will make a change. Honey, all time will do is move on without you.

Listen if you still do not get it, here is an analogy: We all are familiar with checking accounts. How much money you have and how often you make deposits effects your financial decisions. Right? When you get married both your emotional trust accounts are full. This effects your emotional decisions about your spouse and the decisions you make on intimacy, closeness, and trust in your marriage.

For example, if a husband cheats on his wife, he goes into her emotional account and withdraws everything out. So now, she has no trust, no intimacy, no closeness left in her account to use in her marriage. Now, when he does what he needs to do to fix his marriage, he is making deposits back into her account. However, if he does not do like he is supposed to, he continues to pull out of her account so not only are you dealing with an empty account, now your also dealing with a negative balance.

Now, with an empty account all you have to do is fill it. It takes time, but you can quickly see it beginning to fill back up. When you are dealing with a negative balance, you have to pay off the negative before you can start to refill. You can pay and pay and never see increase because of the negative balance.

This is the effect you have on your spouse when you inflict deep wounds from infidelity, affairs, physical, and mental abuse. Some wounds do not withdraw much and they are easier to fix but others drain the account completely. And, like a bank, if the account is left in the negative or empty balance too long, it will be closed.

CHAPTER 7

The Work Never Stops

"Marriage Success is not by accident"

Ok, somewhere, somehow, somebody lied and said, "Once you say "I do" the hard work is over." Let me give you notice that once you say, "I do" is when the hard, real work begins. Two people with different mindsets, different backgrounds, different values, different everything, and you thought it would be easy because you love each other. Now, that is funny!

It is easy to hide our little hiccups under the couch when you are dating. Your hair is always great; your breath always smells good; the cologne or perfume always smells perfect; the food taste great; the apartment is always clean, your clothes are always impeccable, you are always the perfect gentleman or lady. That is easy to do when they are going home in a few hours.

When you say the big "I do," this is when the masks come off. Now you see the hair when they wake up or hanging in the bathroom. The morning breath makes you want to hurl. The cologne or perfume came out of a sample in a magazine. The food was delivered because they cannot cook. You never opened a closet, looked under the couch or under the bed to see all the trash hid there. Manners are out the window and only brought out for company.

You have to love them anyway. In the beginning, it is easy, but, when the fights happen, their little quirks are not so cute anymore. This is where you learn to compromise. When the kids come, you learn to laugh together at the poop on the wall. When the little ones try to pit you against each other, you learn to join forces. When high school and driving starts, you learn to pray together. As you grow older together, you learn to appreciate everyday together.

You learn your best skills in your marriage. You become the best version of yourself in your marriage. You laugh, you cry, you hurt, you heal, you learn, and you live your best life through your marriage. This is why your mistake can only take up a moment. When you drop the baton, you have to pick it up and keep running. No more single races; you are in a relay and you cannot win if each of you do not do your part. Like a relay race, the only way to win is to keep running until you cross that finish line.

There is not one moment when you can quit or everyone loses. You can never stop working. There are no breaks from marriage. There are no vacations from your marital responsibilities. You do not get a pass. How hard you work depends on how important your marriage is to you. You will work from the moment you say "I do" till the moment you take your last breath.

This sounds exhausting and hard, and it **IS** exhausting and hard. But, in the end, you receive trophies of a life well lived, not a marriage lost. A love of your life, not a love lost. A chest full of wonderful memories, not a hole full of regrets. A legacy carried on by your children, not them following in your footsteps.

Either way, you will leave a lasting effect on the next generation. How will you be remembered? What stories will they tell about you?

Everything you do in marriage is purposeful. And, it will always be purposeful. If you put the work in up front, there will be a time when you can just rest and relax in each other. But, if you are one of those that do not take marriage seriously until later, you will still be working hard well into retirement age.

Marriage is one of the most important relationships you will ever have. A decision to marry should never be taken lightly. Lives can be ruined forever. Your children will base their future relationships off what they see of their parent's relationship. The hurt you cause can damage you forever.

You are forever going to be two different people with different mindsets, ideas, feelings, thoughts, emotions, triggers, and you both will always be evolving. Nothing is ever going to just stop and be. When you have children, you expect them to grow and change. Up until the day they move out of your house and into their college dorm, they are changing and evolving. When they get married, they are changing and evolving. When they have children, they are changing and evolving. This never changes until we take our last breath.

So, you have to choose to love your spouse every day. When they make you mad, when they hurt you, when they get fat, when they lose weight, when they lose their job, when they lose all the money, when they get sick, a multitude of changes can occur, and you have to choose to love them despite them all.

Get comfortable in your spouse because you will be there for a while. Or you should be. When my daughter was in elementary school, she would come home saying, "Momma, I hate school." I would immediately tell her to get that thinking out of her spirit because she has too much time left in school to hate it now.

Once you mess your mind up about something, it is hard to fix. Therefore, there are some places you should not allow your mind to wander when you are married. There is always different and better than your spouse out there. That is just the truth. There is always going to be someone handsomer, cuter, have a better body, better hair, bigger breast, tighter buttocks, bigger muscles, better personality, funnier, have more money, a better job, a bigger house, a nicer car, older, younger; it is out there. However, it is not who you chose.

As soon as you purchase your car, as you are driving it off the lot you will see a nicer car. Who turns around and purchases another car? NO ONE. That would be stupid. Be satisfied with your choice. If you choose your spouse like you choose your clothes, you will never be satisfied, and one day when you think you have made the final choice, they will replace you.

It is hard. You are tired, but you chose. You are done. This is it, so make the best of it. I mean it! Your marriage works about as good as you want it to. Put the time in and the effort and it will be great or you can do what you want and be a horrible spouse and you will have a horrible marriage. It really is up to you.

THE WORK NEVER STOPS.
"Marriage Success is not by accident."

CHAPTER 8

Your Happiness is up to You

"How bad do you really want your marriage to work"

I want you to accept this 30-day challenge. Every day for the next 30 days, I want you to put into action every challenge listed in order. Your spouse is not to be involved in any of the planning. **It should all be planned by you and you alone.** Do not involve anyone in this challenge and do not let anyone know what you are doing. This is personal, private, and for your spouse. It is not wise to have spectators. With each challenge come back to the book and journal about what you accomplished, the response you received from your spouse, and how you felt in the process. Do not be discouraged if at first your daily challenges are not well accepted by your spouse. This challenge is in no way a quick fix for your marital problems, but it can help to bring back some of the closeness and intimacy you two have lost. And if you are a new couple with no issues (yet), it will keep the fires-a-burnin...

Day 1

Take some time by yourself to go through old photos of you and your spouse. Chose a favorite photo and have a photo "remake" with your spouse.

_____

_____

_____

_____

_____

_____

_____

_____

_____

_____

_____

_____

_____

Day 2

Go a whole day without thinking or saying anything negative about your spouse

Day 3

Plan a date

_____

_____

_____

_____

_____

_____

_____

_____

_____

_____

_____

_____

_____

Day 4

Think of something you can do to make your spouses day better

Day 5

Give your spouse a compliment
you never have said before

Day 6

Do a house chore you have never done before

_____

_____

_____

_____

_____

_____

_____

_____

_____

_____

_____

_____

_____

_____

_____

Day 7

Ask you spouse's opinion about something meaningful

Day 8

Play a game together

Day 9

Plan a date with another couple (Be yourself)

Day 10

Hug your spouse at least 4 times today

_____

_____

_____

_____

_____

_____

_____

_____

_____

_____

_____

_____

_____

Day 11

Do any outside of the house activity with your spouse today

Day 12

Give your spouse a kiss every time you are in the same room together

Day 13

Ask your spouse to read a Bible verse or poem together and share thoughts on it

_____

_____

_____

_____

_____

_____

_____

_____

_____

_____

_____

_____

_____

_____

Day 14

Make a bucket list together today

Day 15

Compliment your spouse today

Day 16

Do not look at your phone while with your spouse today

Day 17

Touch your spouse on the small of their back every time you are in the room together

Day 18

Make your spouse laugh at least 3 times today

Day 19

Take a walk with your spouse and hold their hand today

Day 20

Plan out a casual date and surprise your spouse by saying, "Let's Go"

Day 21

Leave your spouse a sweet note where you know they will see it today

Day 22

Kiss your spouse in the morning and at night today

Day 23

Take the kids out and tell your spouse you are giving them a personal day

Day 24

Workout together today

Day 25

Plan a picnic, even if it is inside

Day 26

Find your spouse's favorite movie and watch it together

Day 27

Plan a weekend get-a-way

_____

_____

_____

_____

_____

_____

_____

_____

_____

_____

_____

_____

_____

_____

Day 28

Ask your spouse to pray about a weakness you have (Be specific)

_____

_____

_____

_____

_____

_____

_____

_____

_____

_____

_____

_____

_____

Day 29

Surprise your spouse with diner by bringing home your spouse's favorite takeout food

Day 30

Share this book with your spouse. Show them the 30 day journal and talk with them about your feelings. If they are willing, do the challenge over again but this time do it together.

The Rest of Your Lives

Do not let the spontaneity stop after 30 days. Every now and then, surprise your spouse with <u>something</u>. Surprises do not have to be grand or expensive. Just showing your spouse that you are thinking about them and know them well enough to do something you know they would like means a lot. It is nice to know you are appreciated and loved, and when surprised on an ordinary day, well, that just swells the heart.

*Married for over 30 years, I have
laughed, cried, and I learned.
Two people with different mindsets, different
backgrounds, different values, different
everything and you thought it would be easy
because you love each other? Now that is funny!*

It is not over until you quit.

Fix it….

Strengthen it….

& Grow….

TOGETHER.

MARRIAGE IS HARD WORK…
DUUUHHH

Printed in the United States
By Bookmasters